Like our Facebook page
@RiddlesandGiggles

Follow us on Instagram
@RiddlesandGiggles_Official

Questions & Customer Service
hello@riddlesandgiggles.com

Thanksgiving Would You Rather Book for Kids
by Riddles and Giggles™
www.riddlesandgiggles.com

© 2021 Riddles and Giggles™

All rights reserved. This book or parts thereof may not be reproduced in any form, stored in any retrieval system, or transmitted in any form by any means—electronic, mechanical, photocopy, recording, or otherwise—without prior written permission of the publisher, except as provided by United States of America copyright law. For permissions contact: hello@riddlesandgiggles.com

Not for resale. All books, digital products, eBooks and PDF downloads are subject to copyright protection. Each book, eBook and PDF download is licensed to a single user only. Customers are not allowed to copy, distribute, share and/or transfer the product they have purchased to any third party.

FREE BONUS

Get your FREE book download

Christmas Jokes & Would You Rather for Kids

- ✓ Contains a collection of cracking Christmas jokes and Would You Rather Christmas-themed questions

- ✓ More endless giggles and entertainment for the whole family.

Claim your FREE book at www.riddlesandagiggles.com/christmas

Or scan with your phone to get your free download

TABLE OF CONTENTS

Welcome & How to Play... 4
  1. Thanksgiving Origins & Traditions 7
  2. Thanksgiving Dinner 25
  3. Thanksgiving Activities & Fun 53
  4. Fall Fun 71
Before You Go 86
Write Your Own Would You Rather Questions! 88

WELCOME & HOW TO PLAY

Hi there!

Thanksgiving Would You Rather Book for Kids is a collection of funny scenarios, wacky choices, and hilarious situations to choose from.

Some questions might be tricky because they ask you to choose between two good things, such as picking out your favorite candy. But some questions will be challenging because you have to choose between two gross options!

Make sure you take your time and think about which option you prefer—and the reason why!

These questions are fun for all ages and are sure to inspire fun conversations with the whole family.

How to Play

Would You Rather is a fun game that can be played in a group or by yourself.

You are not allowed to answer "neither" or "both"—you must choose an answer!

Remember, there are no right or wrong answers; the aim of the book is to have fun.

If you're playing in a group, ask a question and let everyone think of their answer. As you go around and hear everyone's answer, ask them why they made their choice. Sometimes hearing the reasons behind an answer is just as much fun as asking the questions.

If you take turns, make sure everyone gets a chance to read a question from each section, because some are much sillier than others!

Would you rather play for fun or keep score?

Level up your game so you can determine a winner! This game is tons of fun on its own, but you can also choose to play for points. Adding a layer of guessing gives you a chance to discover who knows the players best. Plus, you'll get a chance to be crowned the winner!

Label each option as A or B. Give players a pencil and piece of paper so they can write down their pick. Before the other players say their answers out loud, the person who read the question will try to guess each player's choice. If they get one right, they get a point! If you play this way, make sure to go around the room, giving every player a chance to be the reader and earn points. Add up all the points at the end of the game. The player who knows everyone the best will be crowned the winner!

This book is a fun game and a great way to learn about each other. But above all, everyone will have tons of fun, and there will be plenty of giggles!

PSST...You can also color the Thanksgiving pictures and use this book as a coloring book AND a Would You Rather question book!

1
THANKSGIVING ORIGINS & TRADITIONS

→ Would you rather be captain of the Mayflower or head cook during the first Thanksgiving?

→ Would you rather volunteer on Thanksgiving at a food bank for people in need or at an animal shelter for animals in need?

→ Would you rather win at pulling the wishbone and have one wish granted on Thanksgiving or get ten wishes granted 20 years from now?

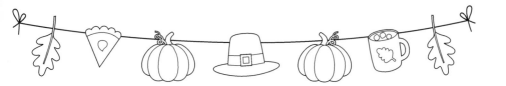

→ Would you rather have giant bowls of candy or giant bowls of chocolate as your Thanksgiving centerpiece?

→ Would you rather never be able to share with your loved ones what you're thankful for or never know what your family is thankful for?

→ Would you rather have to dress in a pilgrim costume for the entire Thanksgiving day or have to dress in a turkey costume?

→ Would you rather celebrate Thanksgiving in the summer instead of fall or celebrate Christmas in the summer instead of winter?

→ Would you rather have to craft one thousand paper turkeys to decorate the Thanksgiving table or have to catch fifty real turkeys to crowd around the Thanksgiving table?

→ Would you rather have a pilgrim travel to the future to join you for Thanksgiving dinner or have an alien travel from space to join you for Thanksgiving dinner?

→ Would you rather have to stand in the crowded line at your favorite store for Black Friday shopping to get a 50% discount or buy online at full price?

→ Would you rather know what the pilgrims were thankful for on their first Thanksgiving or know what your pet is thankful for on Thanksgiving?

→ Would you rather bake 300 cupcakes or 600 chocolate chip cookies to donate to families in need on Thanksgiving?

→ Would you rather be able to spend Thanksgiving with only wild animals or spend Thanksgiving with only stuffed animals?

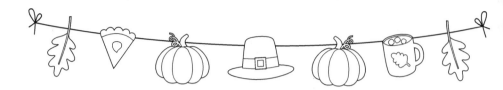

→ Would you rather the lights go out while you're giving thanks or have thunderstorms while you're eating Thanksgiving dinner?

→ Would you rather never be able to celebrate Thanksgiving again or never be able to celebrate Christmas again?

→ Would you rather be able to wear only brown-colored clothes on Thanksgiving Day or wear only orange on Thanksgiving Day?

→ Would you rather have sparkles explode out of your mouth or gobble like a turkey when you try to share what you're thankful for?

→ Would you rather have turkey feathers as hair or have pumpkin seeds as nails?

→ Would you rather have to drive an eight-hour road trip or have a five-hour plane journey to get to your Thanksgiving feast?

→ Would you rather spend Thanksgiving Day with your favorite fictional character or your favorite celebrity?

→ Would you rather have to share what the person sitting next to you is thankful for or have to share what a stranger is thankful for?

→ Would you rather wear the fanciest clothes to Thanksgiving dinner, but they're very uncomfortable, or wear the ugliest clothes, but you feel super comfortable?

→ Would you rather spend your Thanksgiving in the woods with squirrels or at sea with dolphins?

- Would you rather travel back in time to your favorite era to spend Thanksgiving with them or travel into the future to see what Thanksgiving will look like in one hundred years?

- Would you rather have to sing what you're thankful for or have to dance to explain what you're thankful for?

- Would you rather wear pumpkins as shoes or wear a pumpkin as a hat for the entire Thanksgiving Day?

- Would you rather spend Thanksgiving in a different state every year or spend Thanksgiving in a different country every year?

➔ Would you rather always know what Thanksgiving will look like every year or be surprised with new traditions each year?

➔ Would you rather have your birthday be on Thanksgiving or have your birthday be on Christmas?

➔ Would you rather decorate the Christmas tree on Thanksgiving or decorate the Christmas tree on December 1st?

- Would you rather always celebrate Thanksgiving skiing at a ski resort or celebrate Thanksgiving on the beach at a beach resort?

- Would you rather play checkers with a pilgrim or play hopscotch with a pirate?

- Would you rather never be able to celebrate your favorite Thanksgiving tradition ever again or never be able to eat your favorite Thanksgiving food ever again?

→ Would you rather have to go to school on Thanksgiving or have to go to school on Black Friday?

→ Would you rather sleep in on Thanksgiving Day, but you have to go to bed early, or stay up late on Thanksgiving, but you have to wake up early?

→ Would you rather have to dress like a giant corn husk or have to dress like a giant green bean for Thanksgiving?

→ Would you rather spend Thanksgiving with your friends with a Friendsgiving celebration or spend Thanksgiving with your family?

→ Would you rather invite total strangers to your Thanksgiving party, but you get along great, or invite people you know, but the party is very boring?

→ Would you rather write down what you're thankful for and keep it a secret or share with a large group what you're thankful for?

→ Would you rather be in charge of decorations on Thanksgiving Day or be in charge of the music?

→ Would you rather have a Thanksgiving party with beautiful decorations but no food or a Thanksgiving party with ugly and bland decorations but a lot of food?

→ Would you rather wake up on Thanksgiving to find your entire family gobbling like turkeys or wake up to find your entire family oinking like pigs?

- Would you rather never go Black Friday shopping again or never go Christmas shopping again?

- Would you rather never be able to celebrate a modern Thanksgiving, only the way the pilgrims did it, or always have to celebrate a futuristic-themed Thanksgiving?

- Would you rather spend a Thanksgiving in complete silence where nobody can talk or spend Thanksgiving with too much noise?

- Would you rather invite your teachers to your Thanksgiving party or your principal to your Thanksgiving party?

→ Would you rather have to spend Thanksgiving in a country in Europe where they don't celebrate Thanksgiving or spend your Thanksgiving a month earlier in Canada?

→ Would you rather spend your Thanksgiving listening to classical music all day or listening to your parents, grandparents, and older relatives' music all day?

→ Would you rather have a Halloween-themed Thanksgiving dinner or have to dress up like a turkey every year for Halloween?

→ Would you rather wear your pajamas or wear a fancy suit or dress to Thanksgiving every year?

- → Would you rather have an under-the-sea–themed Thanksgiving or have a cowboy-themed Thanksgiving?

- → Would you rather spend Thanksgiving at the North Pole with polar bears or spend Thanksgiving at the South Pole with penguins?

- → Would you rather wear pilgrim shoes or giant clown shoes to Thanksgiving?

→ Would you rather have a dog bark uncontrollably throughout the entire Thanksgiving Day or have a cat hiss throughout the entire Thanksgiving Day?

→ Would you rather explain what you're thankful for or explain what you wish for in the future?

2
THANKSGIVING DINNER

→ Would you rather be able to eat only turkey or be able to eat only ham for every Thanksgiving for the rest of your life?

→ Would you rather go swimming in a pot of salty, savory gravy or take a bath in a bowl of sour and sweet cranberry sauce?

→ Would you rather eat corn straight off of the cob or cut off the kernels and eat them off of the cob? (Watch out if you have braces!)

→ Would you rather have to peel all of the potatoes for mashed potatoes or have to slice all of the bread for stuffing all by yourself?

→ Would you rather share your Thanksgiving meal with your favorite singer, but you can only eat all of your least favorite foods, or eat all of your favorite foods, but you have to turn down an invitation from your favorite singer?

→ Would you rather keep a turkey or a pig as your pet?

→ Would you rather have to eat green beans or broccoli as the only side dish with your Thanksgiving dinner for eternity?

→ Would you rather eat Thanksgiving dinner picnic-style in a park or in a grand indoor ballroom?

THANKSGIVING DINNER

→ Would you rather have apple pie and ice cream for dessert or pumpkin pie and ice cream?

→ Would you rather have Reese's Peanut Butter Cups or M&M's fall from the ceiling during Thanksgiving dinner?

→ Would you rather be in charge of bringing dessert on Thanksgiving or be in charge of bringing the side dishes?

→ Would you rather have all of your guests bring a different meal to Thanksgiving or cook all of your favorite food yourself?

- Would you rather be able to eat only your least favorite part of the turkey for the rest of your life or be able to eat only ham and no turkey for the rest of your life?

- Would you rather be a professional pie taste-tester for a Thanksgiving job or be a professional cake taste-tester?

- Would you rather have to bake all of the desserts or cook the entire dinner for Thanksgiving?

- Would you rather eat Thanksgiving dinner with a talking turkey or with a magical pig that could fly?

THANKSGIVING DINNER

→ Would you rather invite your favorite band/singer to your Thanksgiving dinner or invite all the members of your favorite sports team to your Thanksgiving dinner?

→ Would you rather have an entire Thanksgiving meal made out of just cheese or out of just bread?

→ Would you rather have to eat dog food or have to eat only your least favorite vegetable for Thanksgiving dinner?

→ Would you rather eat your Thanksgiving dinner outside in the freezing cold or eat your Thanksgiving dinner with the heater on so it's boiling hot?

→ Would you rather accidentally spill gravy all over a family member or accidentally fall into a vat of cranberry sauce?

→ Would you rather have to eat Thanksgiving dinner with your least favorite person, but you eat the most delicious food, or eat Thanksgiving dinner with all of your favorite people, but you can't eat any of the food?

→ Would you rather eat a Thanksgiving dinner made entirely of cabbage or made entirely from brussels sprouts?

THANKSGIVING DINNER

→ Would you rather have roasted marshmallows or cinnamon and sugar on top of your sweet potatoes?

→ Would you rather eat the cheesiest mac and cheese or the crispiest French fries with your Thanksgiving dinner?

→ Would you rather eat a bowl of collard greens for breakfast, lunch, and dinner until Christmas or eat a bowl of carrots for every meal until Christmas?

→ Would you rather eat only candy or eat only chicken nuggets for your Thanksgiving meal?

→ Would you rather have singing waiters serve you Thanksgiving dinner or have dancing waiters serve you Thanksgiving dinner?

→ Would you rather eat a pie made out of mustard or a pie made out of ketchup for Thanksgiving?

→ Would you rather have all of your Thanksgiving food grow legs and walk off of your plate or have your Thanksgiving food talk to you?

THANKSGIVING DINNER

→ Would you rather give up your favorite Thanksgiving side dish for the rest of your life or give up your favorite Thanksgiving dessert for the rest of your life?

→ Would you rather have to share your Thanksgiving meal with a family of raccoons or have to share your Thanksgiving meal with a family of friendly bears?

→ Would you rather have to cook Thanksgiving dinner outside without any electricity or get to cook dinner inside, but it's boiling hot while you cook?

→ Would you rather have a magical unicorn or your favorite superhero prepare your Thanksgiving dinner?

- Would you rather find pumpkin seeds coming out of your nose during dinner or find apple seeds coming out of your ears during dinner?

- Would you rather eat roast potatoes or mashed potatoes with your Thanksgiving dinner?

- Would you rather eat chocolate-covered turkey or chocolate-covered ham?

→ Would you rather have all of the vegetables on your Thanksgiving plate magically disappear or be able to eat double the amount of dessert on Thanksgiving?

→ Would you rather have to eat an entire uncooked onion or an entire head of uncooked garlic for your Thanksgiving dinner? Smelly!

→ Would you rather be able to eat only the skins of the potatoes or be able to eat only the stems of broccoli?

→ Would you rather switch Thanksgiving dinners with your dog or not be able to eat anything on Thanksgiving at all?

→ Would you rather eat breakfast food for your Thanksgiving dinner or eat Thanksgiving dinner as your breakfast?

THANKSGIVING DINNER

→ Would you rather have a turkey gobble up your entire Thanksgiving feast or have to eat turkey feed for your Thanksgiving feast?

→ Would you rather eat Thanksgiving dinner by yourself in your favorite fictional destination or with your favorite fictional character in the modern world?

→ Would you rather eat only the dark meat of the turkey for the rest of your life or only the white meat?

→ Would you rather be able to carve the turkey or slice the pies for Thanksgiving dinner?

- Would you rather have to make Thanksgiving dinner with all of your least favorite ingredients or eat Thanksgiving dinner in a room filled entirely with frogs?

- Would you rather have to eat a mediocre Thanksgiving dinner every day for the rest of your life or eat Thanksgiving food only once a year, but it's always the best food you've ever tasted?

- Would you rather eat the most delicious stuffing or eat the most delicious apple pie?

→ Would you rather eat sweet potatoes or white potatoes with your Thanksgiving meal?

→ Would you rather eat a pizza with all Thanksgiving food on it or eat a sandwich with all Thanksgiving food in it?

→ Would you rather eat Thanksgiving dinner with spiders or eat Thanksgiving dinner with slugs?

→ Would you rather eat mac and cheese with no cheese in it or eat sweet potatoes with no marshmallows?

→ Would you rather eat Thanksgiving dinner at a five-star restaurant or your favorite fast-food restaurant?

→ Would you rather have to eat an entire apple core or all of the seeds in a pumpkin?

→ Would you rather eat 4th of July food for Thanksgiving or Thanksgiving food for the 4th of July?

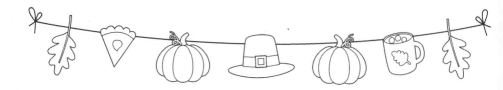

→ Would you rather eat a Thanksgiving dinner made entirely of cookies or brownies?

→ Would you rather eat an apple pie made out of the most sour apples or eat a pumpkin pie made out of rotten pumpkin?

→ Would you rather accidentally burn the turkey or accidentally add too much salt to the mashed potatoes?

→ Would you rather not be able to put any butter on your dinner rolls or not be able to put any gravy on your turkey?

- Would you rather hire a professional chef to make your Thanksgiving dinner or hire a professional baker to bake Thanksgiving dessert?

- Would you rather wake up to find you have no ingredients to make Thanksgiving side dishes or to find you have all the ingredients to make side dishes but there's no turkey?

- Would you rather have to eat pie with no ice cream or have to eat pie with no filling? (That would make for a doughy dessert!

→ Would you rather have cranberry sauce stuck to your foot or have stuffing in your hair for the whole of Thanksgiving Day?

→ Would you rather eat nothing but Halloween candy for your Thanksgiving dinner, but never feel full, or be able to eat only vegetables for Thanksgiving dinner, but you end up feeling satisfied?

→ Would you rather drink an entire pot of gravy or eat the entire turkey all by yourself?

→ Would you rather sleep on a bed of pumpkins or sleep in an apple tree?

→ Would you rather be able to eat only green bean casserole or be able to eat only sweet potato pie for the rest of your life?

→ Would you rather be mistaken for a chef on Thanksgiving Day and have to cook dinner for an entire restaurant or be responsible for catching the turkey for Thanksgiving dinner with your family?

→ Would you rather eat really spicy food with no water for Thanksgiving or eat only sickening-sweet food for Thanksgiving dinner?

→ Would you rather cook an entire Thanksgiving meal that turns out badly or cook a really fantastic Thanksgiving meal that you can't eat a single bite of?

→ Would you rather have to eat pickles with your pumpkin pie or eat onions with your apple pie?

→ Would you rather turn orange from eating too many carrots or turn green from eating too much broccoli?

- Would you rather drink only hot chocolate for the rest of your life or drink only pumpkin spice for the rest of your life?

- Would you rather eat biscuits with gravy or biscuits with butter?

- Would you rather eat pumpkin pancakes for Thanksgiving breakfast or apple dumplings?

➜ Would you rather have to use cinnamon in place of salt or salt in place of cinnamon for Thanksgiving dinner?

➜ Would you rather spend Thanksgiving dinner with a random family in the neighborhood you don't know, but the food is excellent, or spend Thanksgiving dinner with your family and friends, but the food is terrible?

→ Would you rather have to eat an entire Thanksgiving meal made out of salad or have to eat an entire Thanksgiving meal made out of fish?

→ Would you rather eat Thanksgiving dinner with a family of friendly vampires or eat Thanksgiving dinner with a family of friendly ghosts?

→ Would you rather eat an entire pumpkin pie with your hands tied behind your back or eat an entire turkey with just your feet?

THANKSGIVING DINNER

→ Would you rather have food on your face during Thanksgiving dinner, but nobody tells you, or have food stuck in your teeth, but nobody tells you?

→ Would you rather eat a bowl of candy corn or a bowl of lollipops as your Thanksgiving dinner?

→ Would you rather have apple fritters without any apples for dessert or chocolate cupcakes without any frosting for dessert?

→ Would you rather drink your favorite drink only on Thanksgiving or drink nothing but your favorite drink every day for the rest of your life?

→ Would you rather have Thanksgiving dinner take twice as long to cook but taste twice as good or have Thanksgiving dinner take only minutes to cook but tastes just ok?

→ Would you rather eat a home-cooked meal on Thanksgiving or go to a restaurant?

→ Would you rather try a new cuisine on Thanksgiving or stick to tradition?

3
THANKSGIVING ACTIVITIES & FUN

→ Would you rather participate in a turkey trot with real turkeys or participate in a polar bear plunge with real polar bears?

→ Would you rather take a nap after Thanksgiving dinner or go for a walk?

→ Would you rather watch football all afternoon on Thanksgiving or play video games?

→ Would you rather curl up after Thanksgiving with a good book or have a dance party in your living room?

→ Would you rather have to take your Thanksgiving nap next to your snoring grandpa or have to sit next to your annoying cousin during Thanksgiving dinner?

→ Would you rather score a winning touchdown in an NFL Thanksgiving Day football game or be able to dance in Macy's Thanksgiving Day parade?

→ Would you rather play a board game or play a card game on Thanksgiving?

THANKSGIVING ACTIVITIES & FUN

→ Would you rather never be able to watch your favorite TV show on Thanksgiving or never be able to play your favorite game on Thanksgiving?

→ Would you rather teach your family a simple TikTok dance or perform a difficult TikTok dance by yourself in front of your family on Thanksgiving?

→ Would you rather have to watch the same movie on a loop throughout the whole of Thanksgiving Day, or have to listen to the same song for the whole of Thanksgiving Day?

→ Would you rather forget your lines while singing in a Thanksgiving Day parade or trip over your own feet while dancing in a Thanksgiving Day parade?

→ Would you rather watch a football game on TV or watch it in person?

→ Would you rather have to decorate your Christmas tree on Thanksgiving using only Thanksgiving-themed decorations or have to decorate your Thanksgiving table using only Christmas-themed decorations?

→ Would you rather design the float for a Thanksgiving parade or be the grand marshal of the parade?

→ Would you rather make candy apples or bake apple pies on Thanksgiving?

→ Would you rather get lost in a corn maze or a pumpkin patch and not make it to Thanksgiving dinner?

→ Would you rather never be able to go Black Friday shopping ever again or never be able to watch another football game ever again?

→ Would you rather train for a turkey trot only for it to get canceled the day of or cook Thanksgiving dinner only for all your guests to cancel?

→ Would you rather have to learn a new instrument to play the day of the Thanksgiving Day parade or have to play in a football game without ever playing football?

THANKSGIVING ACTIVITIES & FUN

→ Would you rather decorate pumpkins on Thanksgiving or go bobbing for apples?

→ Would you rather make candy apples or bake apple pies on Thanksgiving?

→ Would you rather deal with crowded stores on Black Friday or be stuck in a crowded football stadium on Thanksgiving?

→ Would you rather be in the marching band or be a dancer in the Thanksgiving parade?

→ Would you rather act out a Thanksgiving play at school in front of your classmates or act out a Thanksgiving play at home in front of your family?

→ Would you rather play chess against a chess master on Thanksgiving or play cards against a magician?

→ Would you rather never be able to take a walk after Thanksgiving dinner ever again or never be able to take a nap after Thanksgiving dinner ever again?

THANKSGIVING ACTIVITIES & FUN

→ Would you rather have to crawl on all fours for an entire turkey-trot or have to stand while watching an entire football game on TV?

→ Would you rather have to wear a giant tutu while playing a football game or have to wear a full football uniform while dancing in a Thanksgiving parade?

- Would you rather lose your favorite board game on Thanksgiving so you spend the whole day bored, or spend Thanksgiving without any electricity?

- Would you rather spend Thanksgiving with your favorite TikTok personality or spend Thanksgiving with your favorite actor?

- Would you rather get lost in a forest during your Thanksgiving Day walk or get lost in a crowded mall on Black Friday?

- Would you rather accidentally sleep through the turkey-trot or accidentally sleep through the football game on Thanksgiving?

→ Would you rather have to walk a five-mile walk with a gobbling turkey by your side or have to walk a five-mile walk with a chirping bird by your side?

→ Would you rather take a nap that lasts from Thanksgiving to Christmas or stay awake from Thanksgiving to Christmas?

→ Would you rather go clothes shopping or go toy shopping on Black Friday?

- Would you rather receive a gift on Thanksgiving or give a gift to someone else?

- Would you rather bake pumpkin cupcakes or apple cookies on Thanksgiving?

- Would you rather eat leftovers on Black Friday or cook something new?

- Would you rather take your Thanksgiving nap in front of the TV or in complete silence?

- Would you rather feel overly full on Thanksgiving or be too hungry?

→ Would you rather go Black Friday shopping early in the morning or sleep in?

→ Would you rather play an outdoor sport with your family on Thanksgiving or do an indoor puzzle?

→ Would you rather spend Thanksgiving in the rain or in the sunshine?

→ Would you rather complete a scavenger hunt on Thanksgiving or read a book?

→ Would you rather have the turkey go missing on Thanksgiving or have the TV stop working on Thanksgiving?

→ Would you rather be a football commentator on TV or a football player?

→ Would you rather go to someone else's house for Thanksgiving or have people come to your house?

→ Would you rather have a cookie-eating contest or have a cupcake-eating contest on Thanksgiving?

→ Would you rather spend Thanksgiving with pirates or Vikings?

→ Would you rather read or listen to music during a long road trip to Thanksgiving dinner?

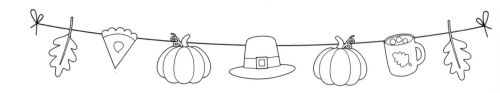

→ Would you rather have your history teacher recite to you a five-hour lecture on the history of Thanksgiving or be the one to watch the turkey for five hours while it roasts?

→ Would you rather win the lottery on Thanksgiving or be drafted into your favorite football team and play on Thanksgiving?

→ Would you rather go to an amusement park on Thanksgiving or go to a concert?

→ Would you rather learn to drive so that you can drive your family to your Thanksgiving destination or learn to fly a plane to fly your family to Thanksgiving?

→ Would you rather sleep over at someone's house or have other people sleep over at your house for Thanksgiving?

→ Would you rather teach someone from another country about Thanksgiving or have someone from another country teach you about their traditions?

→ Would you rather have an outdoor bonfire on Thanksgiving or light an indoor fireplace?

→ Would you rather always be bored on Thanksgiving, but the food is always great, or always have really bad tasting food, but you're always entertained?

4

FALL FUN

→ Would you rather be able to drink only pumpkin spice lattes or only hot chocolate for the rest of your life?

→ Would you rather have to take a spoonful of cinnamon or have to stuff five marshmallows in your mouth?

→ Would you rather get lost in a corn maze or in a forest at midnight?

→ Would you rather wear a squash as a hat or wear an apple seed necklace?

→ Would you rather go pumpkin picking or apple picking?

→ Would you rather go to a fall fair or go to a fall farmer's market?

→ Would you rather live in a world where fall doesn't exist or live in a world where spring doesn't exist?

→ Would you rather have to go into a freezing cold swimming pool on a chilly fall day or have to go into a very hot tub on a warm summer day?

→ Would you rather eat caramel apples or candy apples?

→ Would you rather swim in a pool made out of caramel sauce or go trampolining on a bed of marshmallows?

→ Would you rather go bobbing for apples or go on a fall-themed scavenger hunt?

→ Would you rather lose your taste buds, so you'll never be able to taste your favorite fall treats again, or lose the season of fall altogether?

→ Would you rather have fall or summer all year round?

- Would you rather have a scarecrow or a jack-o'-lantern come to life and be your best friend?

- Would you rather have to sleep on a bale of hay for the entire fall season or have to sleep on a bed of corn husks?

- Would you rather spend your fall on a deserted island or in the Arctic tundra?

- Would you rather fall off of a hayride or trip over a pumpkin in front of all your friends?

→ Would you rather live on a farm or live in a downtown apartment building in the fall?

→ Would you rather rake leaves during the fall or mow the lawn during the summer?

→ Would you rather magically turn into a scarecrow or magically turn into a pumpkin?

→ Would you rather make snow angels in a pile of leaves or make snow angels in snow?

→ Would you rather make a treehouse to sit in during a fall day or make a pillow fort indoors to hang out in during a fall day?

→ Would you rather go camping during the fall or go camping during the summer?

→ Would you rather attend an outdoor concert during the fall or an outdoor funfair during the fall?

→ Would you rather endure a rainy fall day with no boots or rain jacket or attend a Halloween party with no costume?

→ Would you rather have a fall that was full of snow or have a fall that was full of sunshine?

→ Would you rather have all of the corn in the corn maze come to life and start telling jokes or have all of the hay on your hayride come to life and start singing?

- Would you rather walk on stilts while apple picking, so you're able to pick apples from the tallest tree, or pick the perfect pumpkin while pumpkin picking?

- Would you rather drink hot chocolate with no whipped cream or eat apple pie with no ice cream?

- Would you rather spend your fall with a pack of wolves or spend it with a family of grizzly bears?

- Would you rather live in a world where fall doesn't exist, but there's sunshine all the time, or live in a world that has only fall, but it's always dark?

- Would you rather go out on a crisp fall morning to chop wood or rake leaves?

- Would you rather wake up early or sleep in during the fall?

→ Would you rather be chased by a giant turkey or be chased by a giant corn husk?

→ Would you rather make your own Halloween costume or buy it?

→ Would you rather turn orange like a pumpkin every time you eat a pumpkin or turn red like an apple every time you eat an apple?

→ Would you rather have your birthday in the fall or the summer?

→ Would you rather drink freezing cold hot chocolate or eat a caramel apple with caramel that is just too hard?

→ Would you rather learn to knit your own fall blanket or learn to bake your own fall pie?

→ Would you rather drive the tractor that leads the hayride or be a passenger on the hayride?

→ Would you rather plant an apple seed and watch it grow into an enormous apple tree, or plant a pumpkin seed and watch it grow into an enormous pumpkin patch?

→ Would you rather go to school in the summer and have a vacation in the fall, or go to school in the fall and keep a vacation in the summer?

FALL FUN

→ Would you rather find the perfect apple, but you can't eat it, or find the perfect pumpkin, but you can't carve it?

→ Would you rather get rid of bugs in the summertime and have a fall full of bugs or keep bugs in the summertime and enjoy fall without any bugs?

→ Would you rather eat a pumpkin that gives you superpowers or have a magical scarecrow that gets you whatever you want?

BEFORE YOU GO

Did you have fun with those sometimes corny, sometimes silly, sometimes even gross, Would You Rather questions?

Now that you have gotten the hang of it, spend some time thinking up your own Would You Rather questions! To make them extra thought-provoking, customize your questions according to family traditions or fun things you do with your friends.

Remember to make the game even more fun by asking people to share their reasons for choosing one option over another. Often, hearing the reasons behind the choices is the most fun part of the game because you learn how people think!

If you want to make this game a tradition, consider keeping score so you can look back on it for years to come.

You can also play Would You Rather games for any holiday, celebration, or theme. Think about any characters or traditions involved with the holiday, and you will be able to come up with more questions.

Once you think of the questions, you can play the game anywhere! It is great to play on long road trips, at school, or even when waiting in line at the grocery store.

Would You Rather questions are even fun to ask when you are meeting new people or if you can't think of anything to talk about.

Have fun coming up with your own questions, getting to know each other, and being as silly as possible!

WRITE YOUR OWN WOULD YOU RATHER QUESTIONS!

Have fun coming up with your own questions to play with your friends and family!

WRITE YOUR OWN WOULD YOU RATHER QUESTIONS!

WRITE YOUR OWN WOULD YOU RATHER QUESTIONS!

WRITE YOUR OWN WOULD YOU RATHER QUESTIONS!

WRITE YOUR OWN WOULD YOU RATHER QUESTIONS!

WRITE YOUR OWN WOULD YOU RATHER QUESTIONS!

WRITE YOUR OWN WOULD YOU RATHER QUESTIONS!

WRITE YOUR OWN WOULD YOU RATHER QUESTIONS!

COLLECT THEM ALL!

Thanksgiving Joke Book for Kids

Thanksgiving Would You Rather Book for Kids

www.riddlesandgiggles.com

Made in the USA
Middletown, DE
21 November 2021